Too Old For Summer Camp And Too Young To Retire

A New Shoe Book

Jeff MacNelly

St. Martin's Press / New York

Design by Glen M. Edelstein

Library of Congress Cataloging-in-Publication Data

MacNelly, Jeff.
  [Shoe., Selections]
  Too old for summer camp and too young to retire : a new Shoe book by Jeff MacNelly.
      p.   cm.
  Selections from the comic strip.
  ISBN 0-312-01822-3 (pbk.) : $5.95
  I. Title.   II. Title: Shoe.
PN6728.S475M345   1988
741.5'973—dc19   87-36722
                                                              CIP

Too Old For Summer Camp And Too Young To Retire

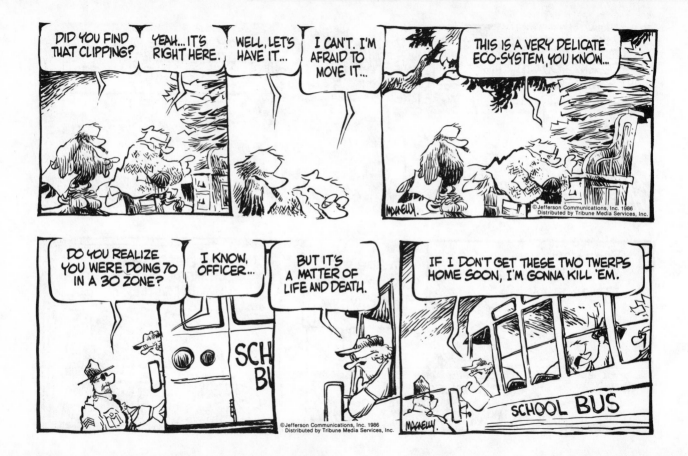

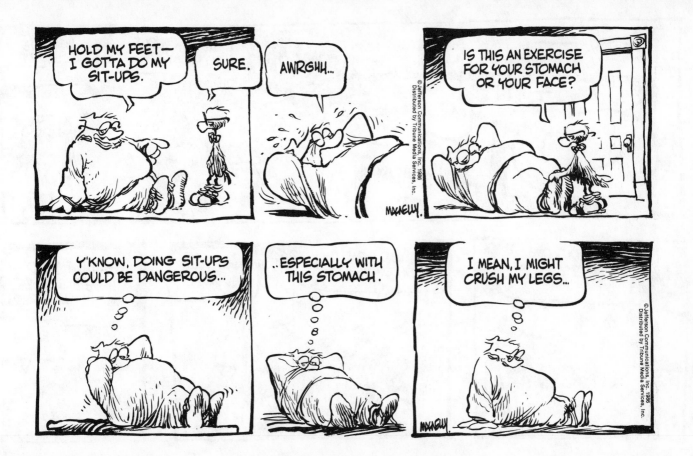

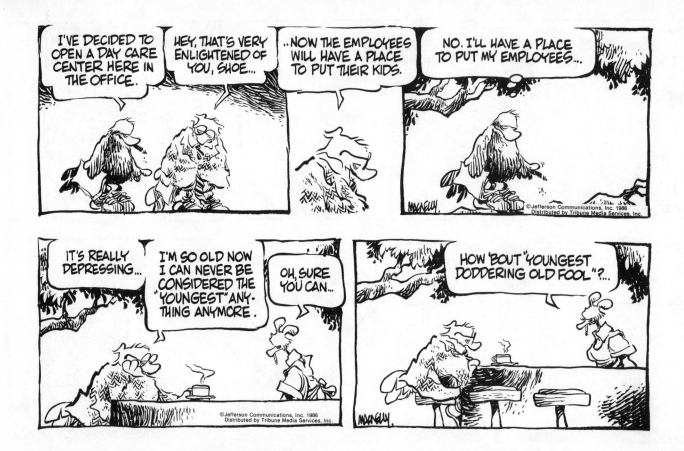

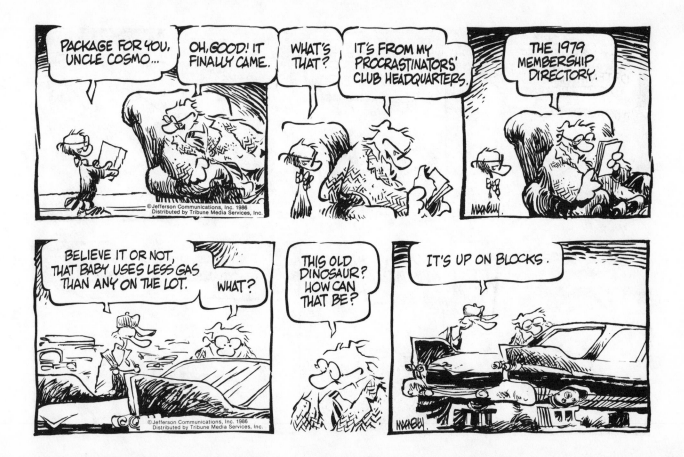

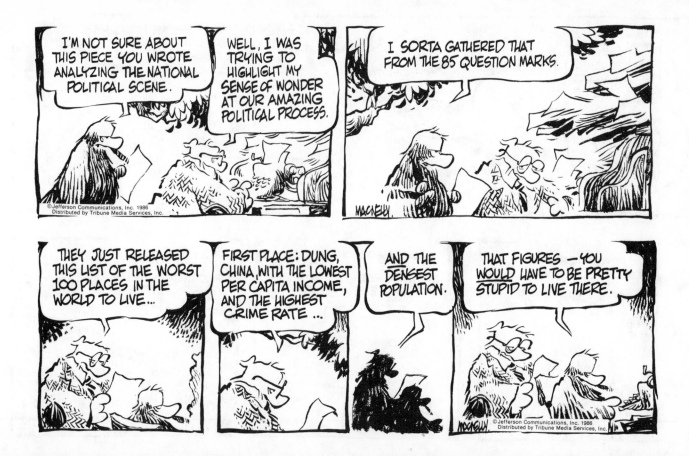

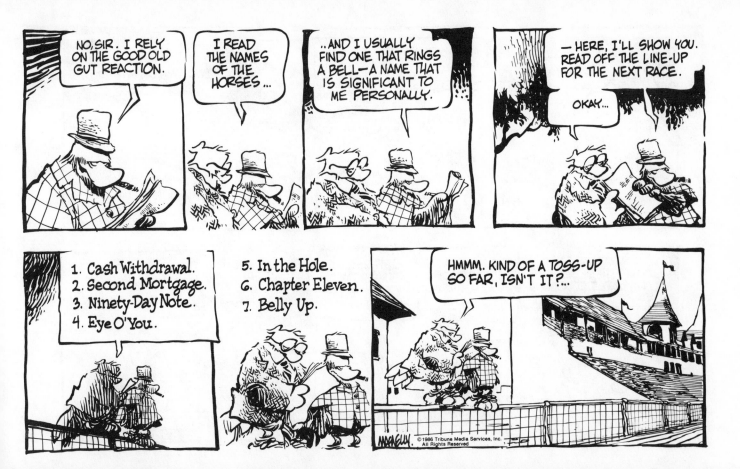

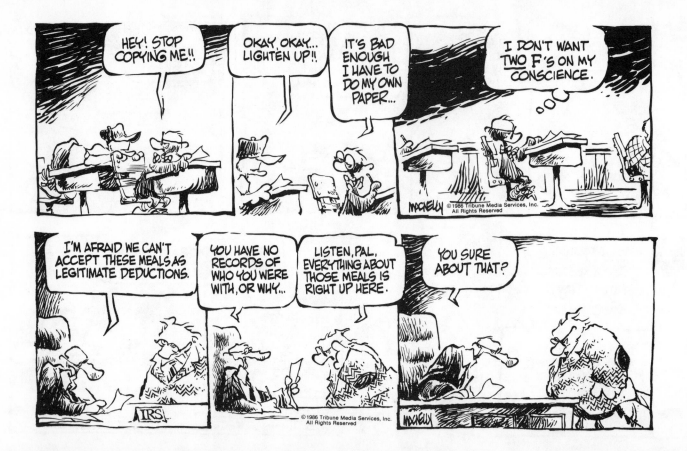

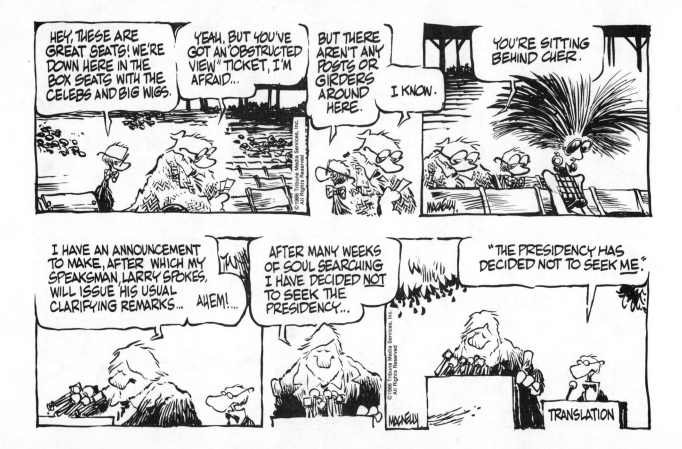

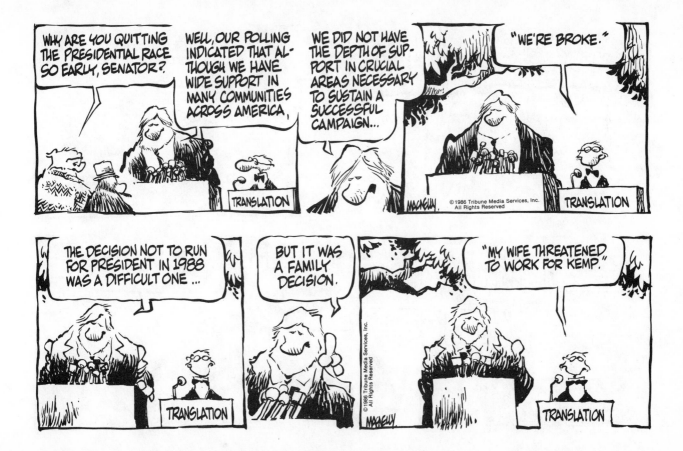

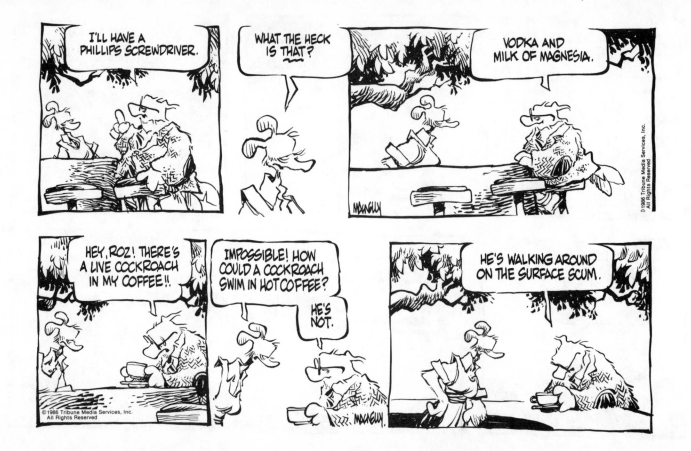

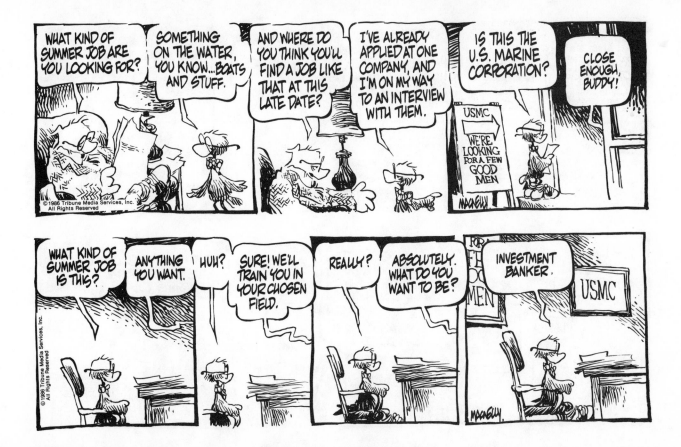

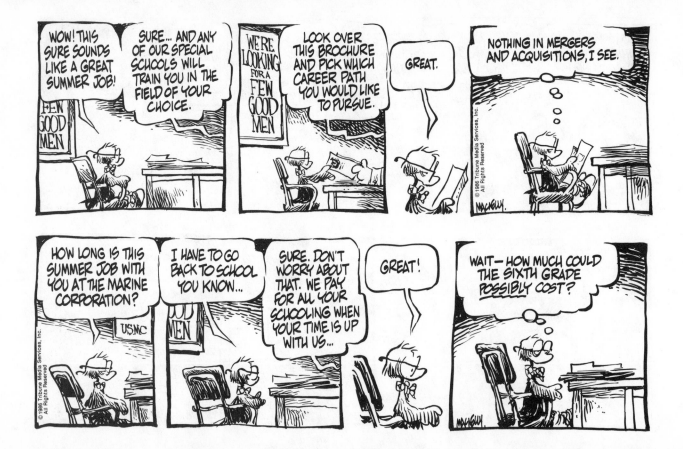

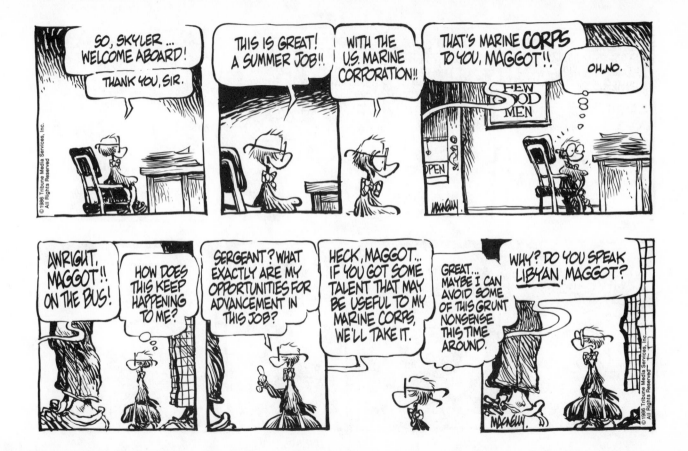

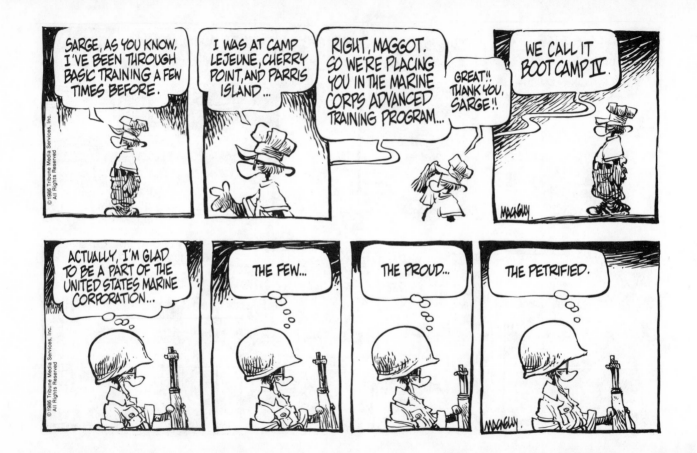

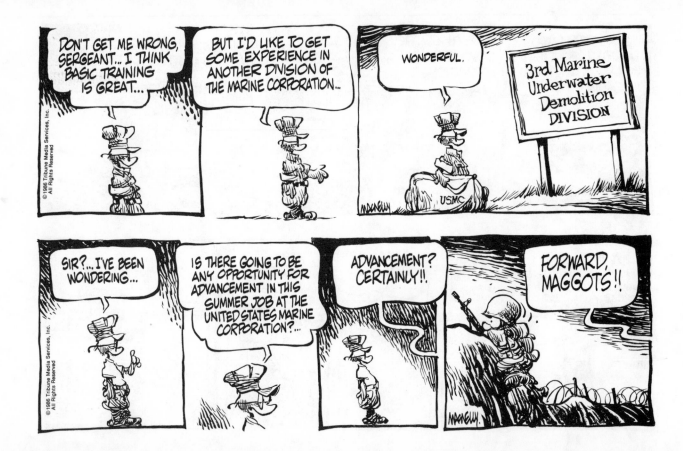

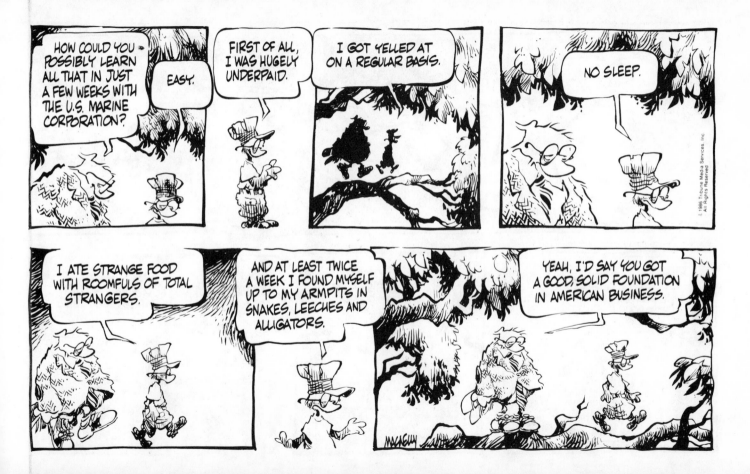

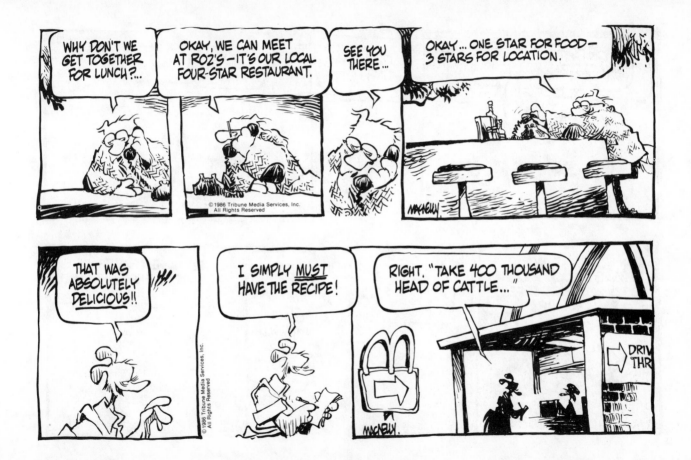

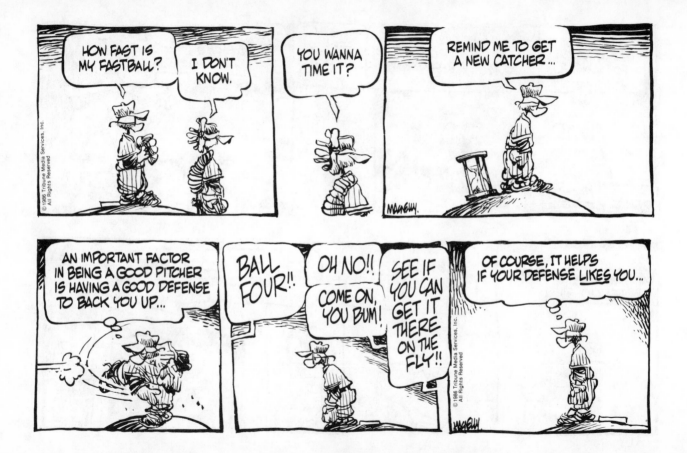

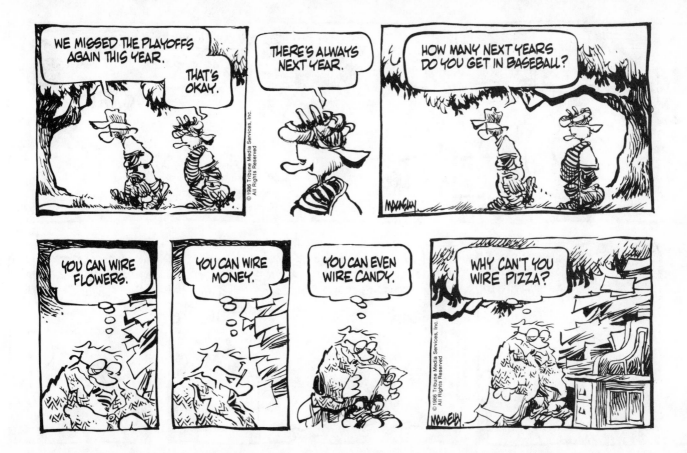

Shoe
By Jeff MacNelly
DID YOU BUY THAT BLUE SHIRT FOR THE TV CAMERAS, SENATOR?
HEAVENS, NO... IT WAS A GIFT.
FROM MY MAKE-UP GIRL.
NOW THAT THEY'RE TELEVISING THE SENATE SESSIONS, HAVE THINGS CHANGED, SENATOR?
NOT REALLY, FELLAS...
U.S. SENATORS ARE USED TO TELEVISION.

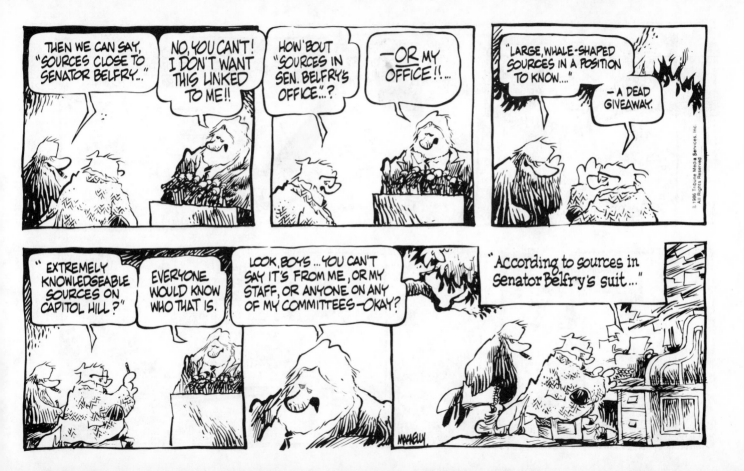

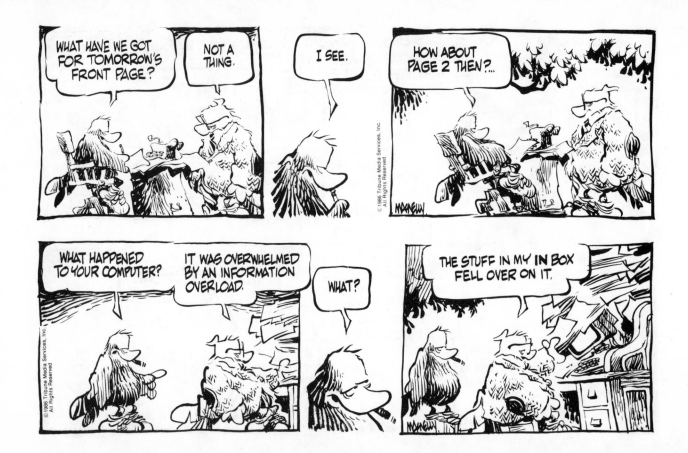

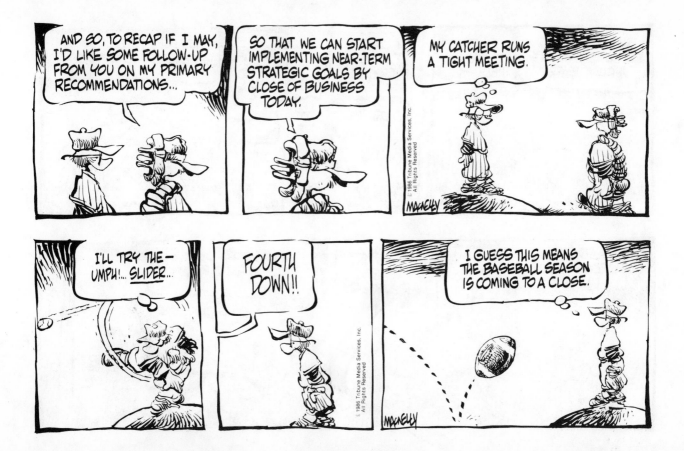

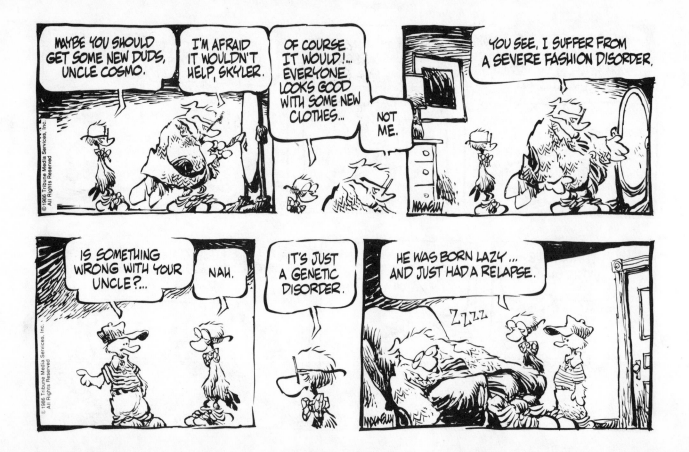

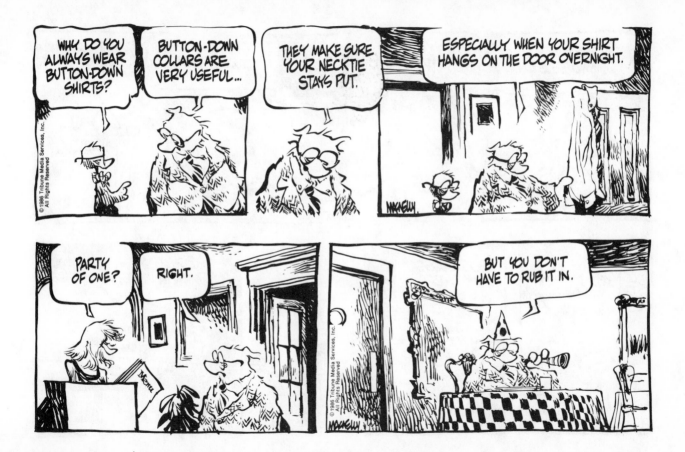

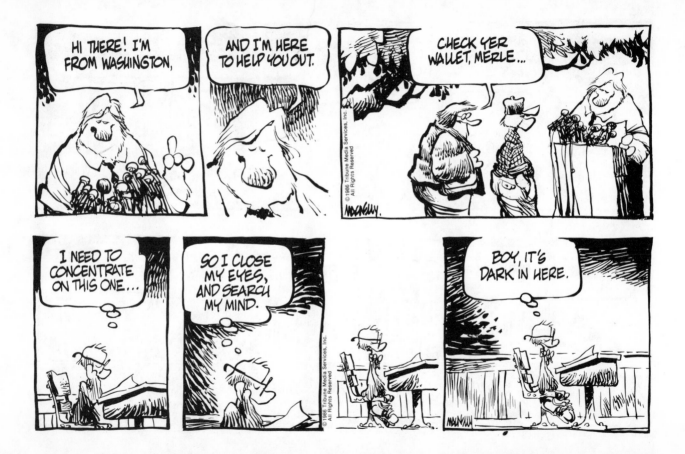

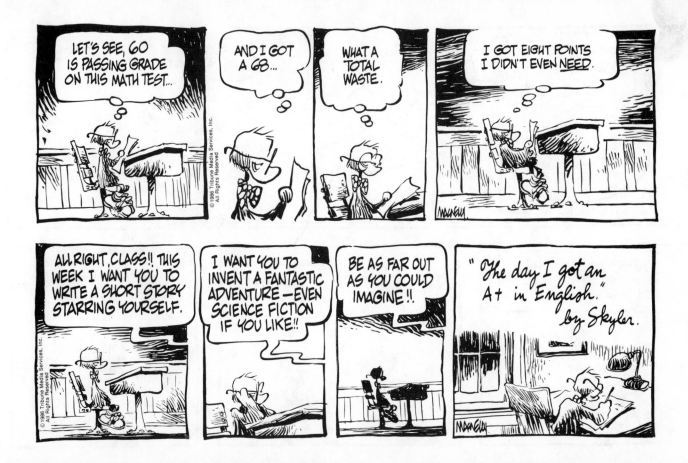

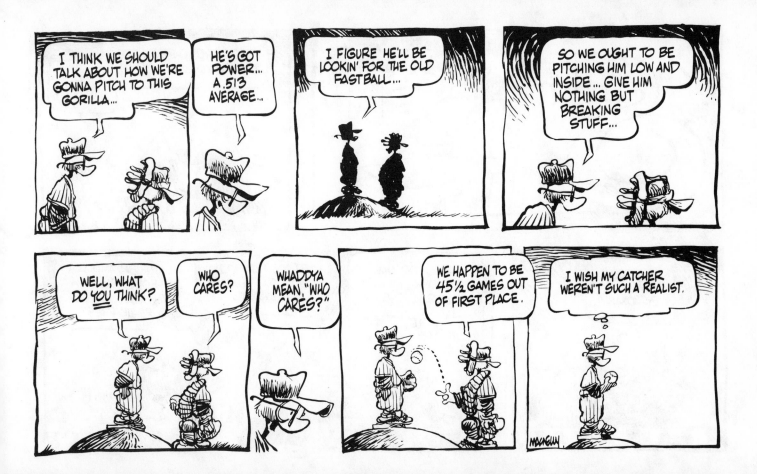

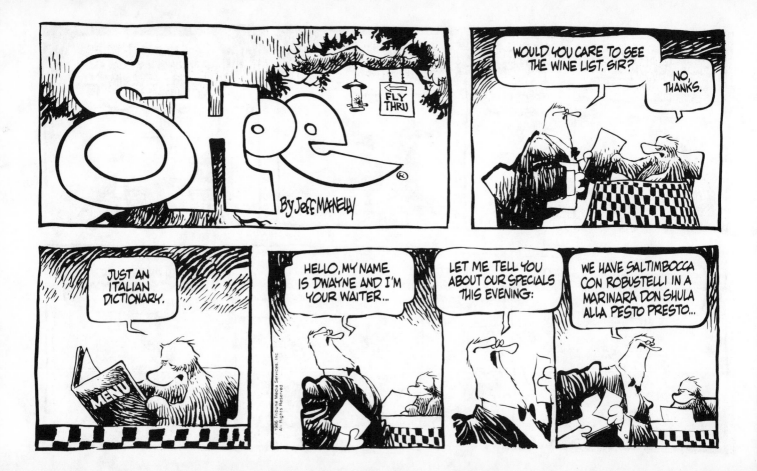

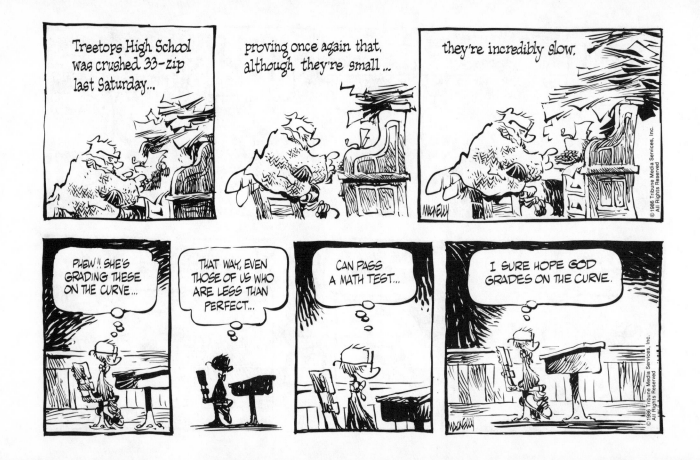

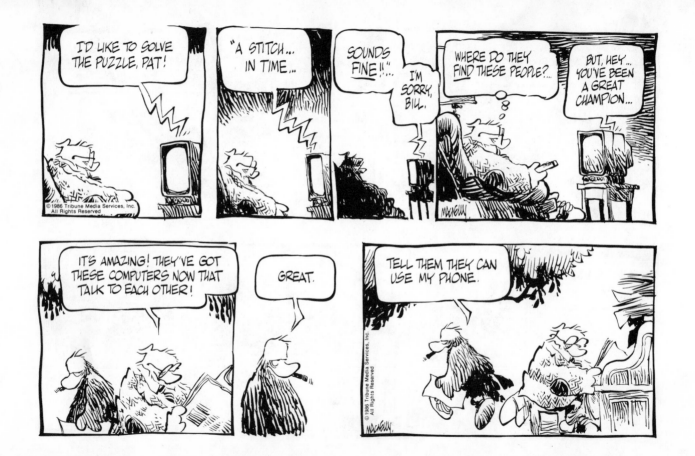

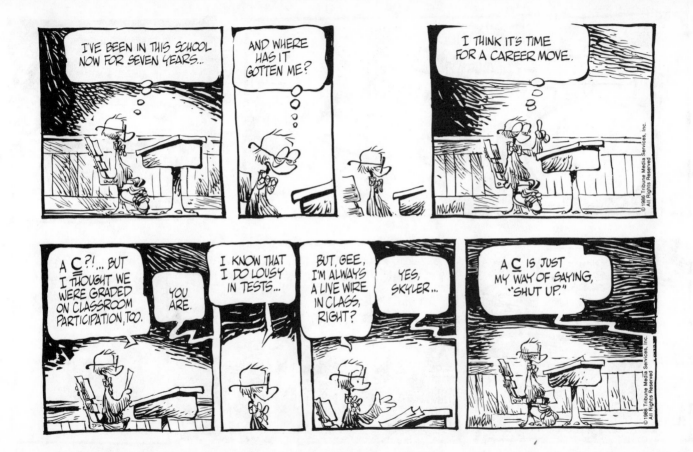

I ran past Teddy Roosevelt and his Rough Riders preparing for their famous charge up Hamburger Hill!
As I made my way past our tanks, I knew this would be a turning point in the Civil War...
So I knew Grant's message had to be very important.
© 1986 Tribune Media Services, Inc All Rights Reserved
To get safely back from the front I had to avoid Confederate reconnaissance aircraft, and maintain total radio silence, of course....
Finally, I reached the gates of the Union stronghold...
As I waved at my old buddies Jim Bowie, Davy Crockett and John Wayne, I hurried to General Grant's tent.
YOU HAVE A MESSAGE FOR ME, SIR?
YES.... HERE, SON...
A C MINUS?
NICE TRY, KID...
MACNELLY

Shoe
By Jeff MacNelly
THERE'S THE MAGNIFICENT MARY BETH MALARKEY... CHEERING HER GUTS OUT...
AND I'M SITTING HERE ON THE BENCH.
I'LL NEVER GET A CHANCE TO IMPRESS HER
A MINUTE TO PLAY, WE'RE DOWN BY FIVE POINTS, I'M ON THE BENCH, AND MARYBETH MALARKEY DOESN'T KNOW I EXIST.
SKYLER! GET IN THERE!
A HUSH FALLS OVER THE CROWD HERE IN PASADENA... AS THE QUARTERBACK GOES UP TO THE LINE....

© 1986 Tribune Media Services, Inc.
All Rights Reserved

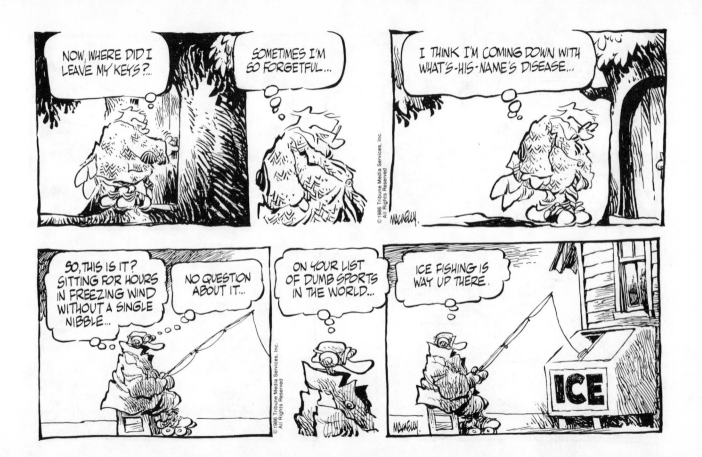

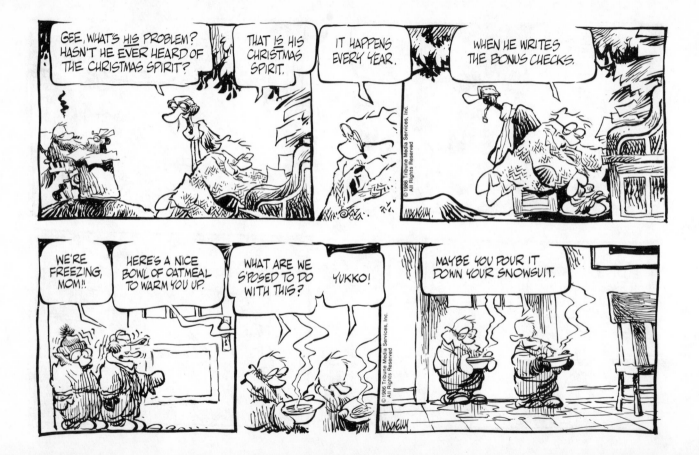

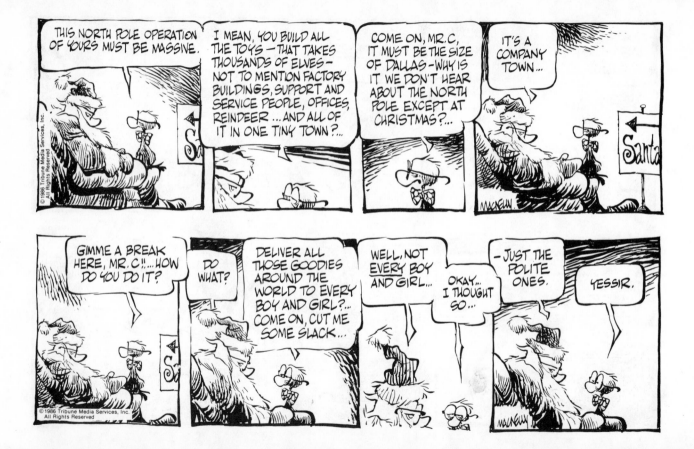

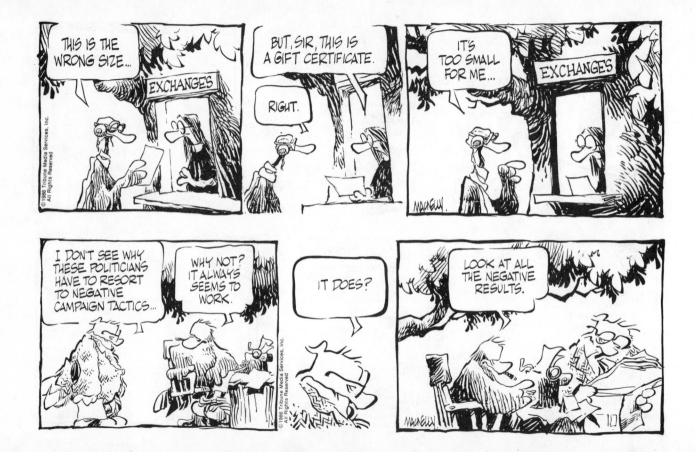